HOME MAINTENANCE
LOG BOOK

——THIS BOOK BELONGS TO——

Name : ....

Address : ....

....

SSIONAL AME	PHONE	COMPANY
n		
an		
e		
System		
es		
Siding		
ers Insurance		
ers System		
noval		
able/Satellite		
ers Association		
ownship		
ecinct		

...IONAL ...ME	PHONE	COMPANY N...
...stem		
...ing		
...Insurance		
...System		
...val		
...e/Satellite		
...Association		
...nship		
...nct		

SSIONAL AME	PHONE	COMPANY
n		
an		
e		
System		
es		
Siding		
ers Insurance		
ers System		
noval		
able/Satellite		
ers Association		
ownship		
ecinct		

IONAL ME	PHONE	COMPANY N
stem		
ng		
Insurance		
System		
val		
e/Satellite		
Association		
nship		
nct		

JANUARY

FEBRUARY

MA[RCH]

APRIL

MAY

J[UNE]

JULY

AUGUST

SEPT[EMBER]

[O]CTOBER

NOVEMBER

DECE[MBER]

Water Heater	Electrical Box

Hvac Units	Water Meter & Min Shu...

...er & Maib Shut-Off	Sprinkler Controls

...oke Detectors	Fire Extinguishers

Water Heater	Electrical Bo

Hvac Units	Water Meter & Min

Meter & Maib Shut-Off	Sprinkler Contr

Smoke Detectors	Fire Extinguish

Water Heater	Electrical Box

Hvac Units	Water Meter & Min Sh[ut-Off]

[Wa]ter & Maib Shut-Off	Sprinkler Controls

[Sm]oke Detectors	Fire Extinguishers

Water Heater	Electrical Box

Hvac Units	Water Meter & Min

Meter & Maib Shut-Off	Sprinkler Contr

Smoke Detectors	Fire Extinguishe

Water Heater	Electrical Box

Hvac Units	Water Meter & Min Shut

ter & Maib Shut-Off	Sprinkler Controls

moke Detectors	Fire Extinguishers

Water Heater	Electrical Bo[x]
Hvac Units	Water Meter & Min
[Water] Meter & Maib Shut-Off	Sprinkler Contr[ol]
Smoke Detectors	Fire Extinguish[er]

Water Heater	Electrical Box

Hvac Units	Water Meter & Min Shu[t-Off]

[Wat]er & Maib Shut-Off	Sprinkler Controls

[Sm]oke Detectors	Fire Extinguishers

Water Heater	Electrical Bo[x]

Hvac Units	Water Meter & Min

[Gas] Meter & Maib Shut-Off	Sprinkler Cont[rol]

Smoke Detectors	Fire Extinguish[er]

Water Heater	Electrical Box

Hvac Units	Water Meter & Min Sh

ter & Maib Shut-Off	Sprinkler Controls

noke Detectors	Fire Extinguishers

Water Heater	Electrical Box

Hvac Units	Water Meter & Min

Meter & Maib Shut-Off	Sprinkler Contr

Smoke Detectors	Fire Extinguishe

Water Heater	Electrical Box

Hvac Units	Water Meter & Min Shut

er & Maib Shut-Off	Sprinkler Controls

oke Detectors	Fire Extinguishers

Water Heater	Electrical Bo...

Hvac Units	Water Meter & Min...

...Meter & Maib Shut-Off	Sprinkler Cont...

Smoke Detectors	Fire Extinguish...

System / Appliance	Problem

System / Appliance	Problem

System / Appliance	Problem

System / Appliance	Problem

System / Appliance	Problem

System / Appliance	Problem

System / Appliance	Problem

System / Appliance	Problem

System / Appliance	Problem

System / Appliance	Problem

System / Appliance	Problem

	System / Appliance	Problem

System / Appliance	Problem

	System / Appliance	Problem

System / Appliance	Problem

System / Appliance	Problem

System / Appliance	Problem

System / Appliance	Problem

System / Appliance	Problem

	System / Appliance	Problem

System / Appliance	Problem

System / Appliance	Problem

System / Appliance	Problem

System / Appliance	Problem

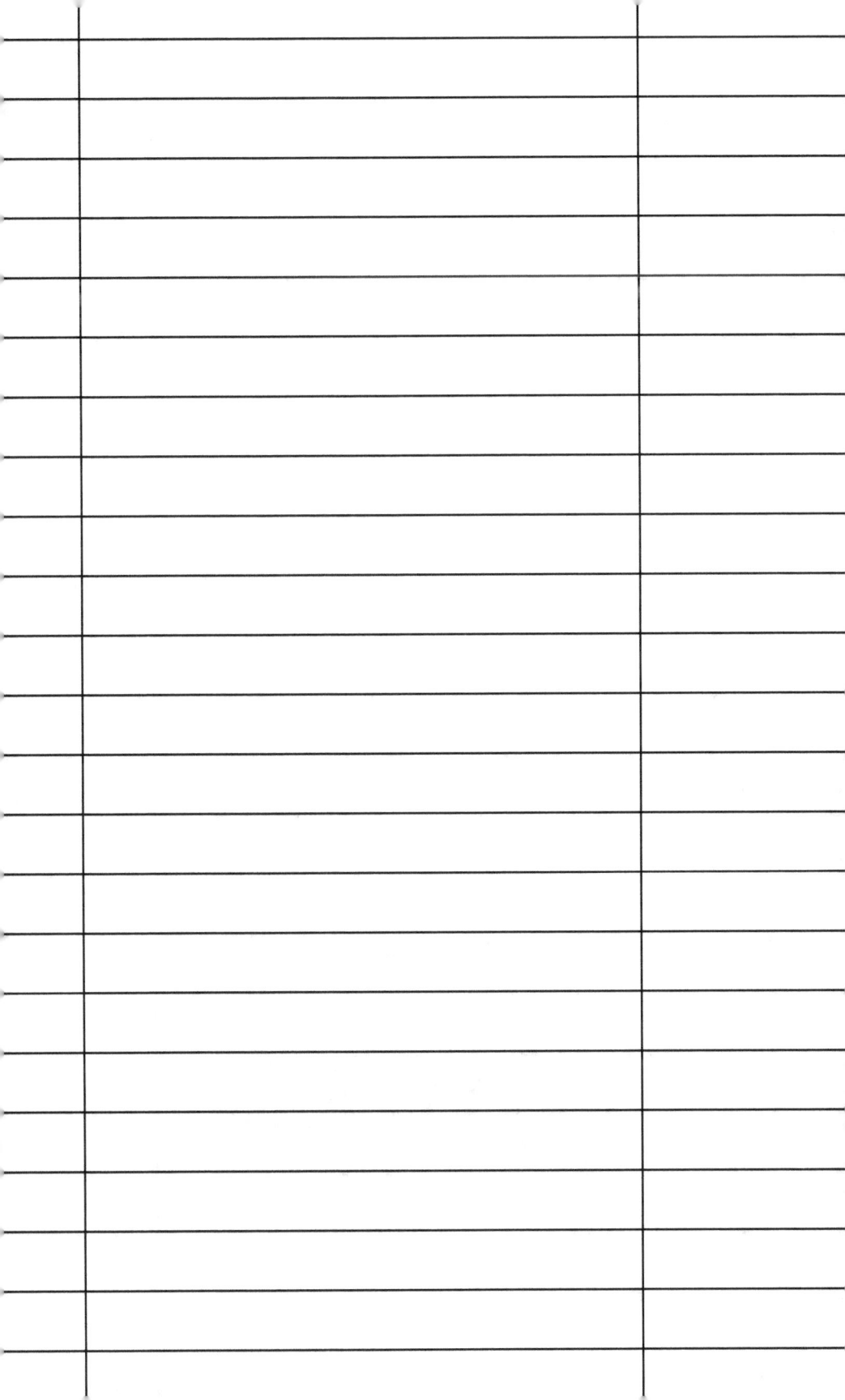

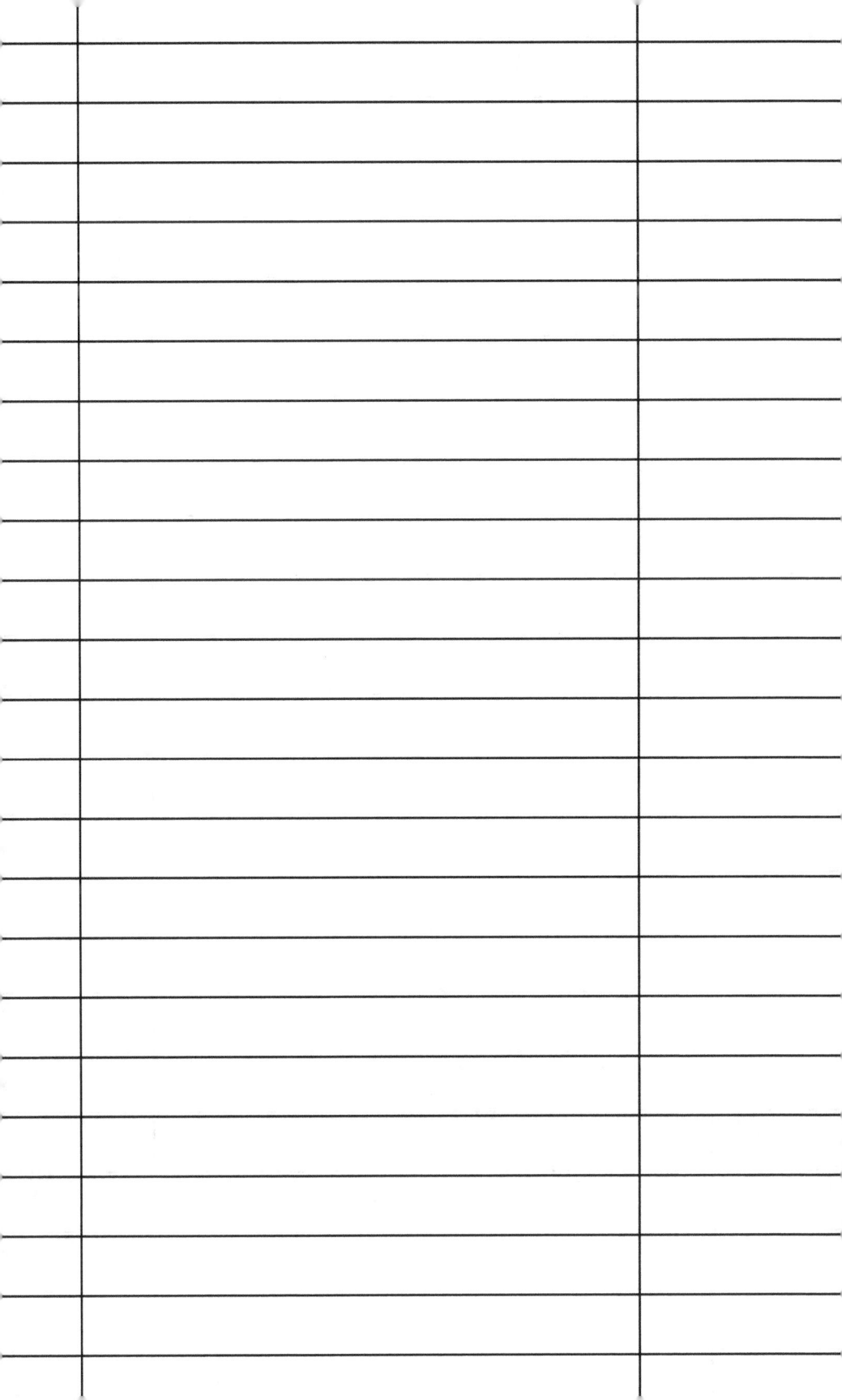

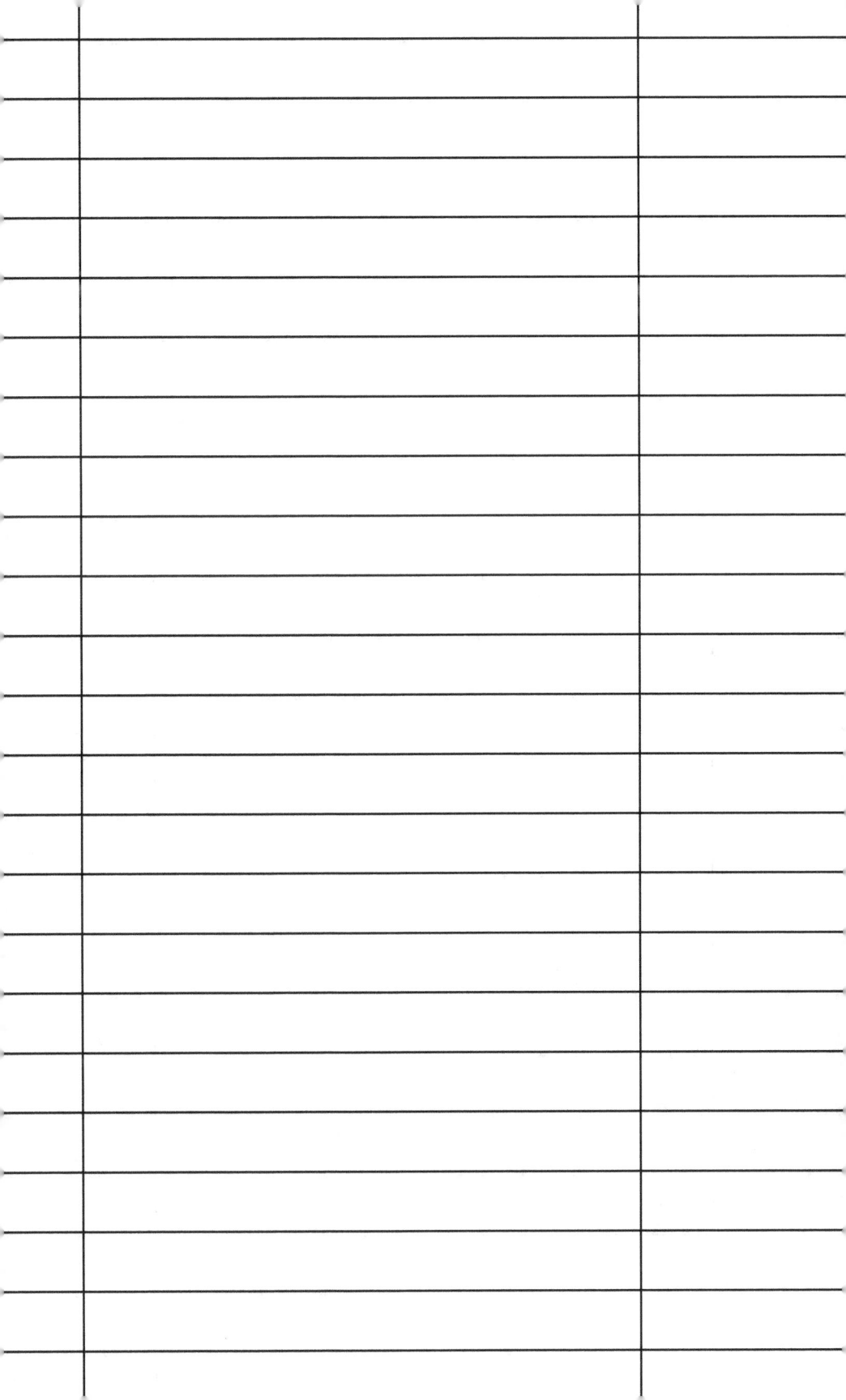

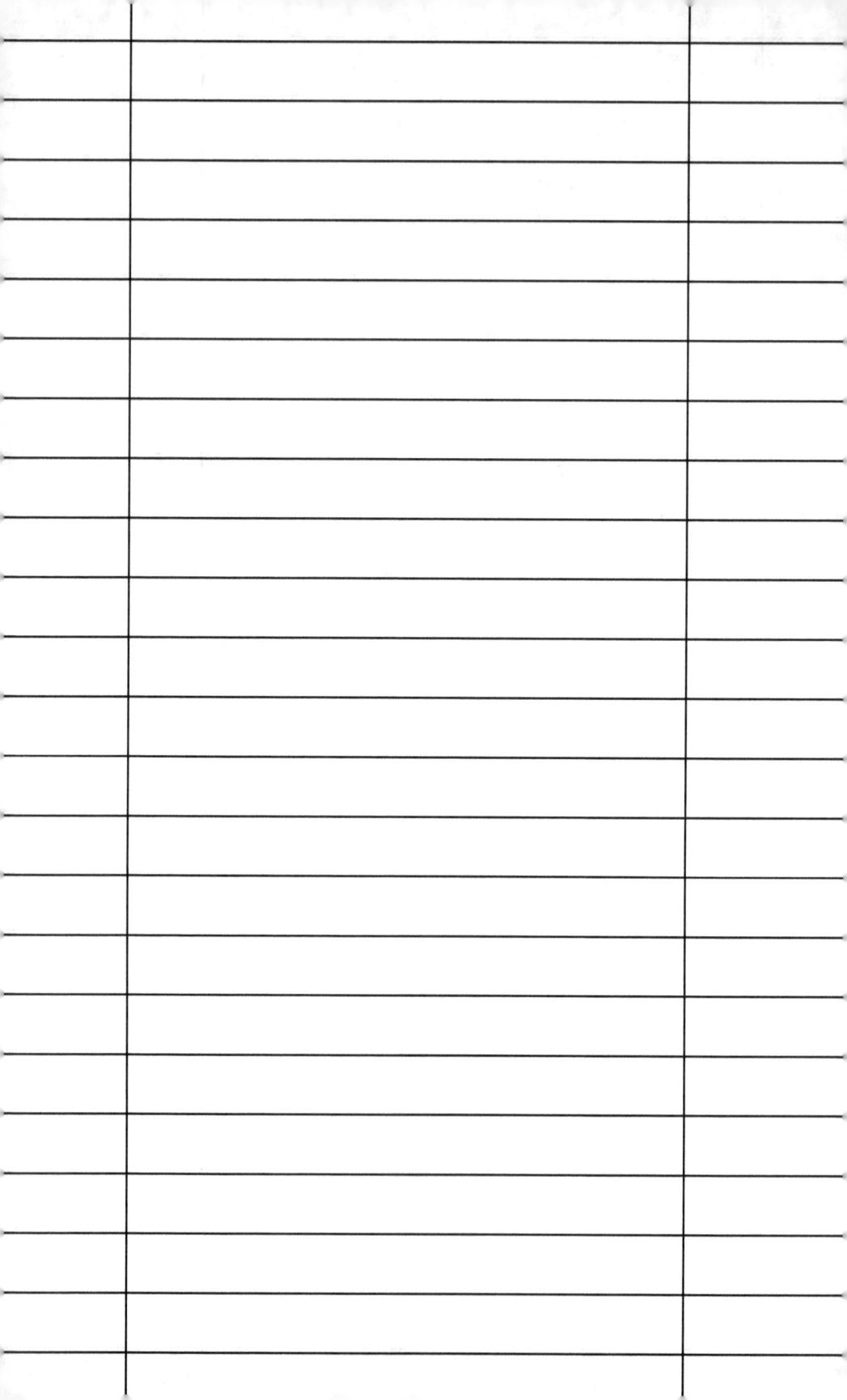

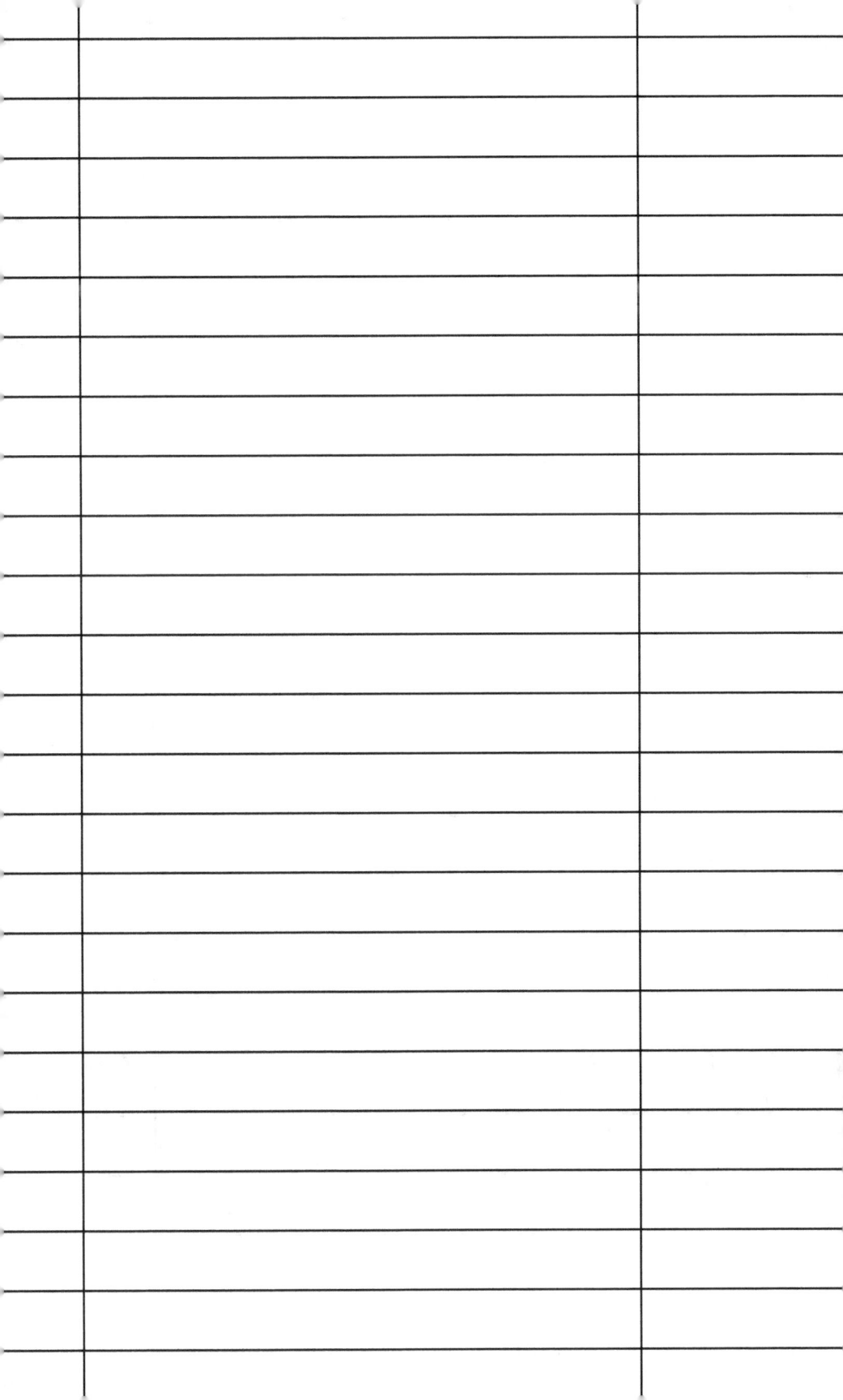

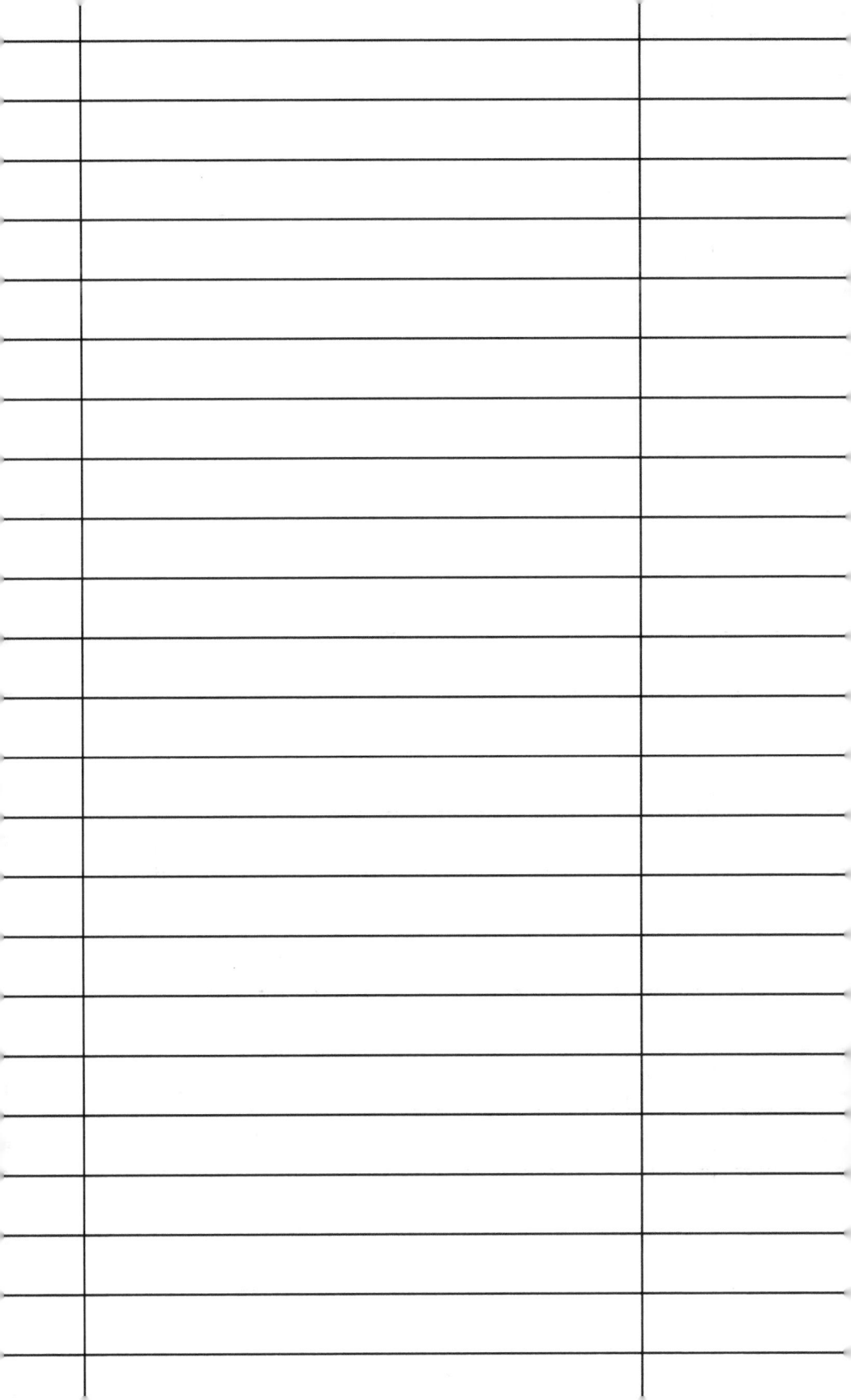

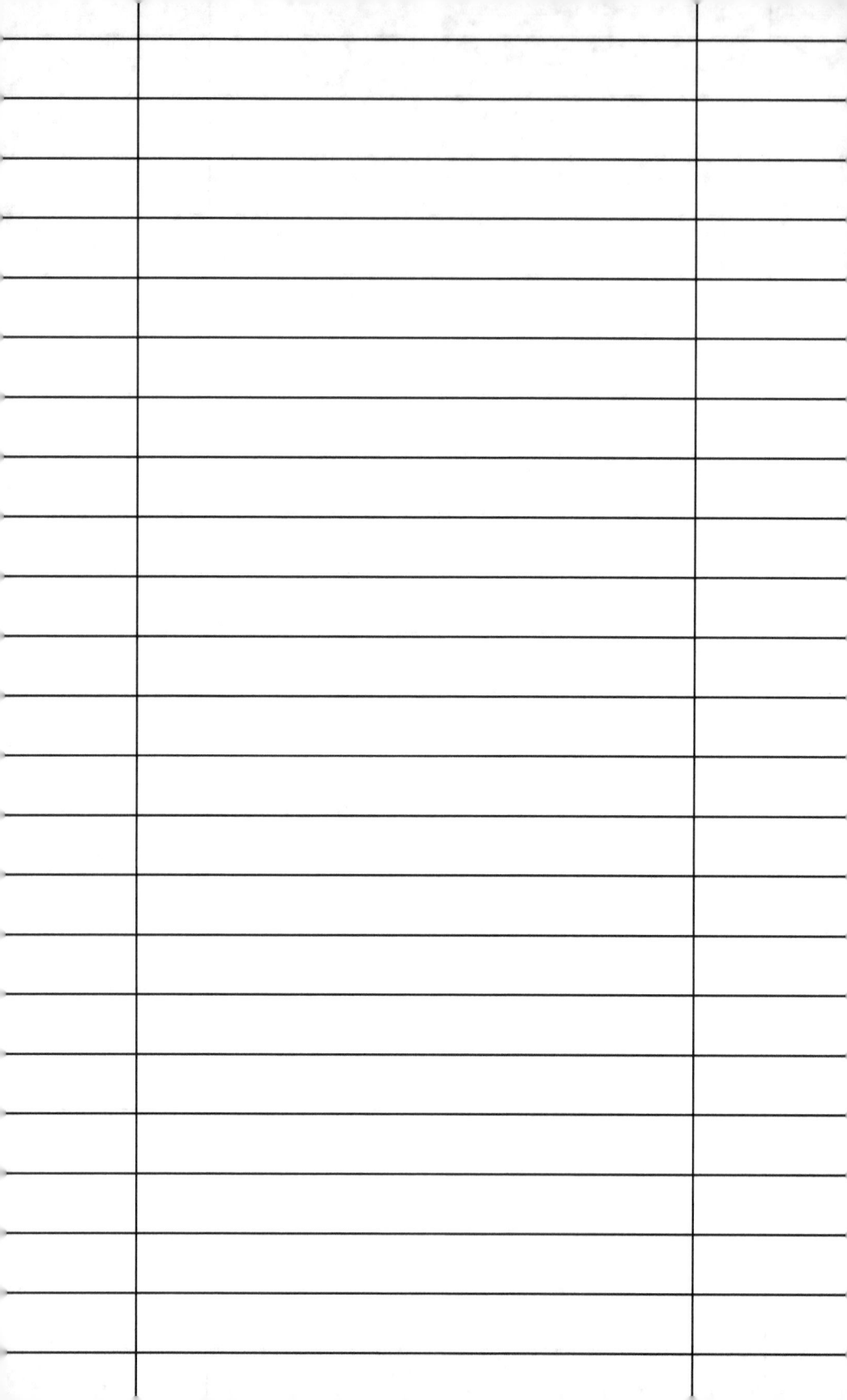

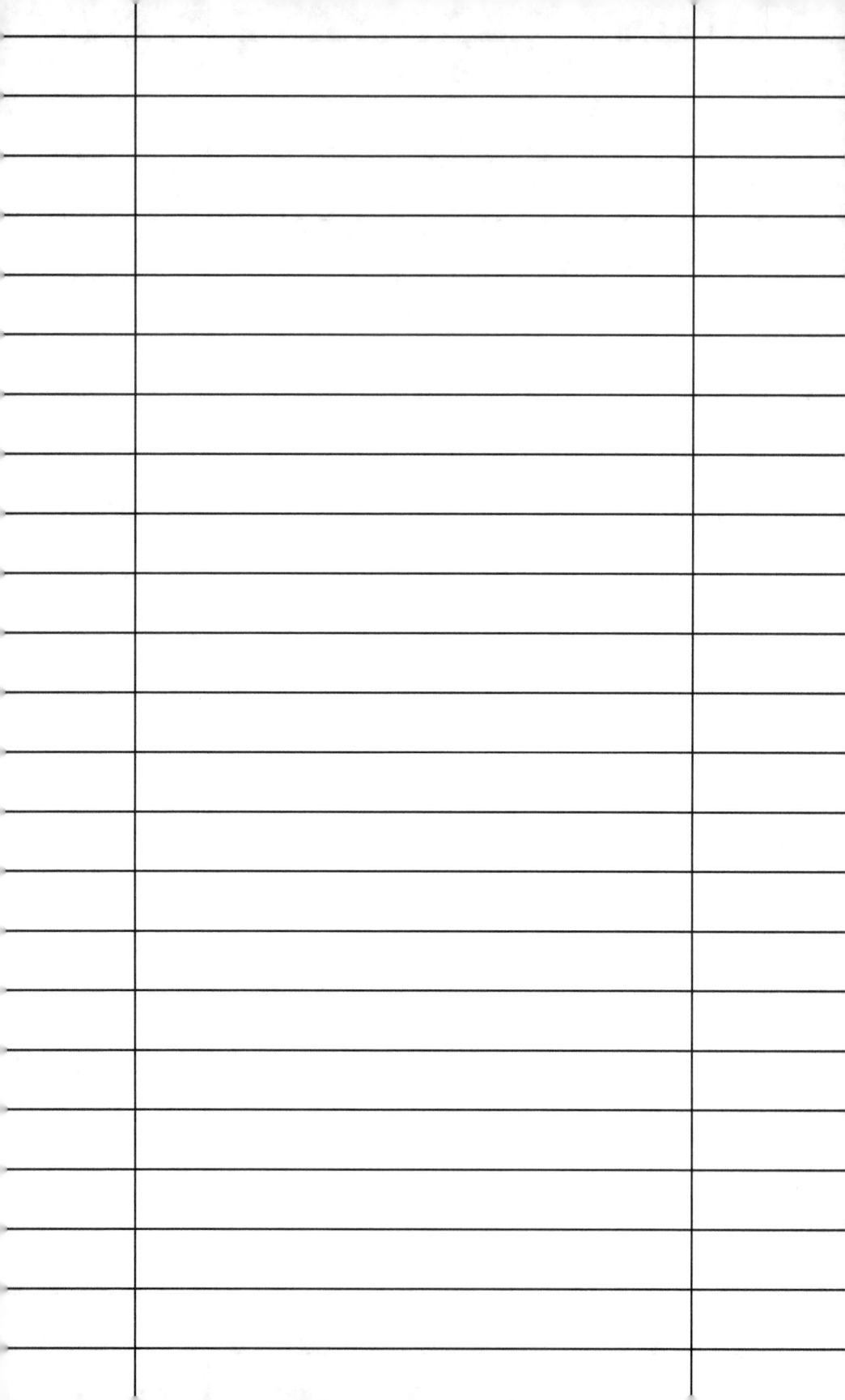

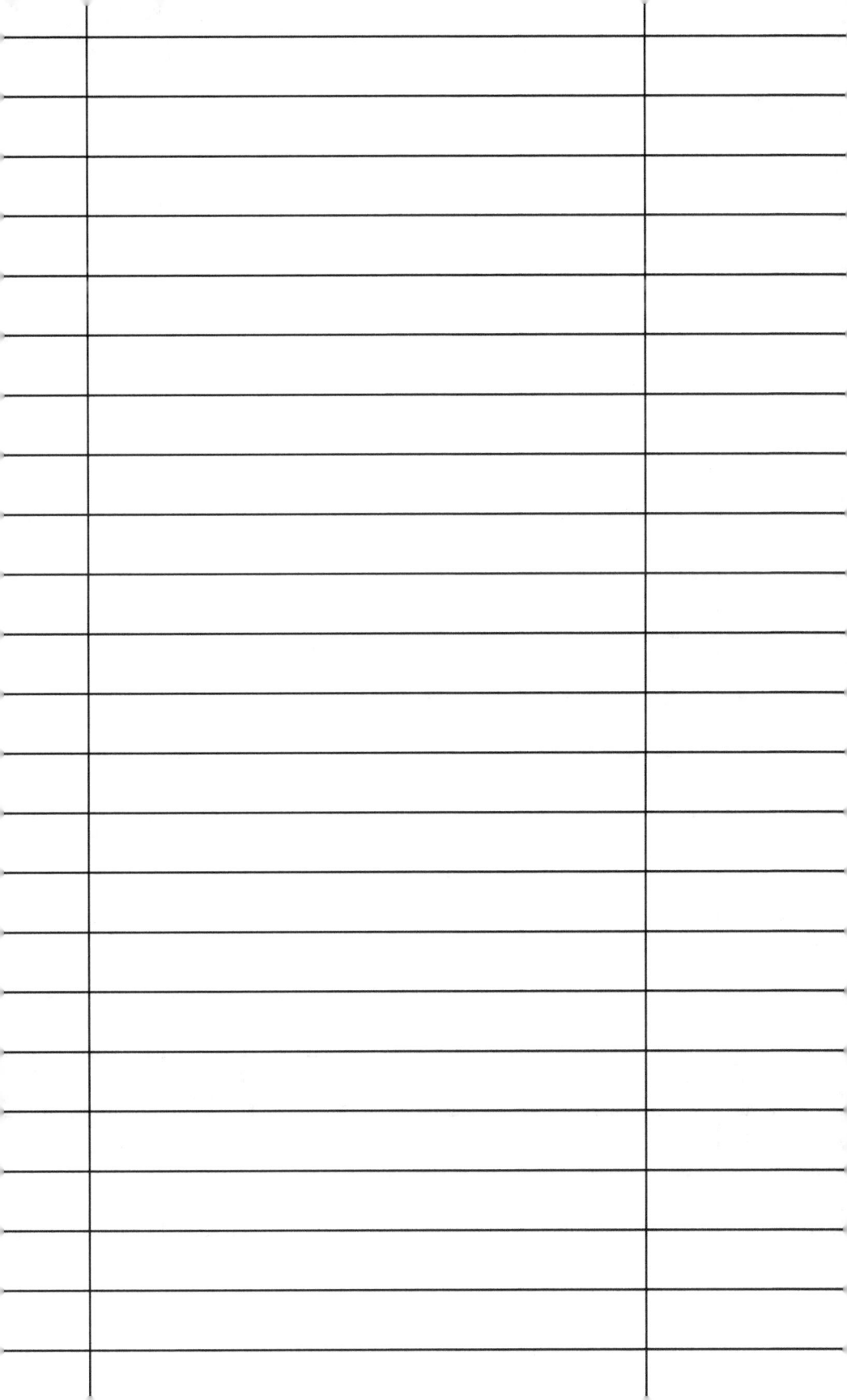

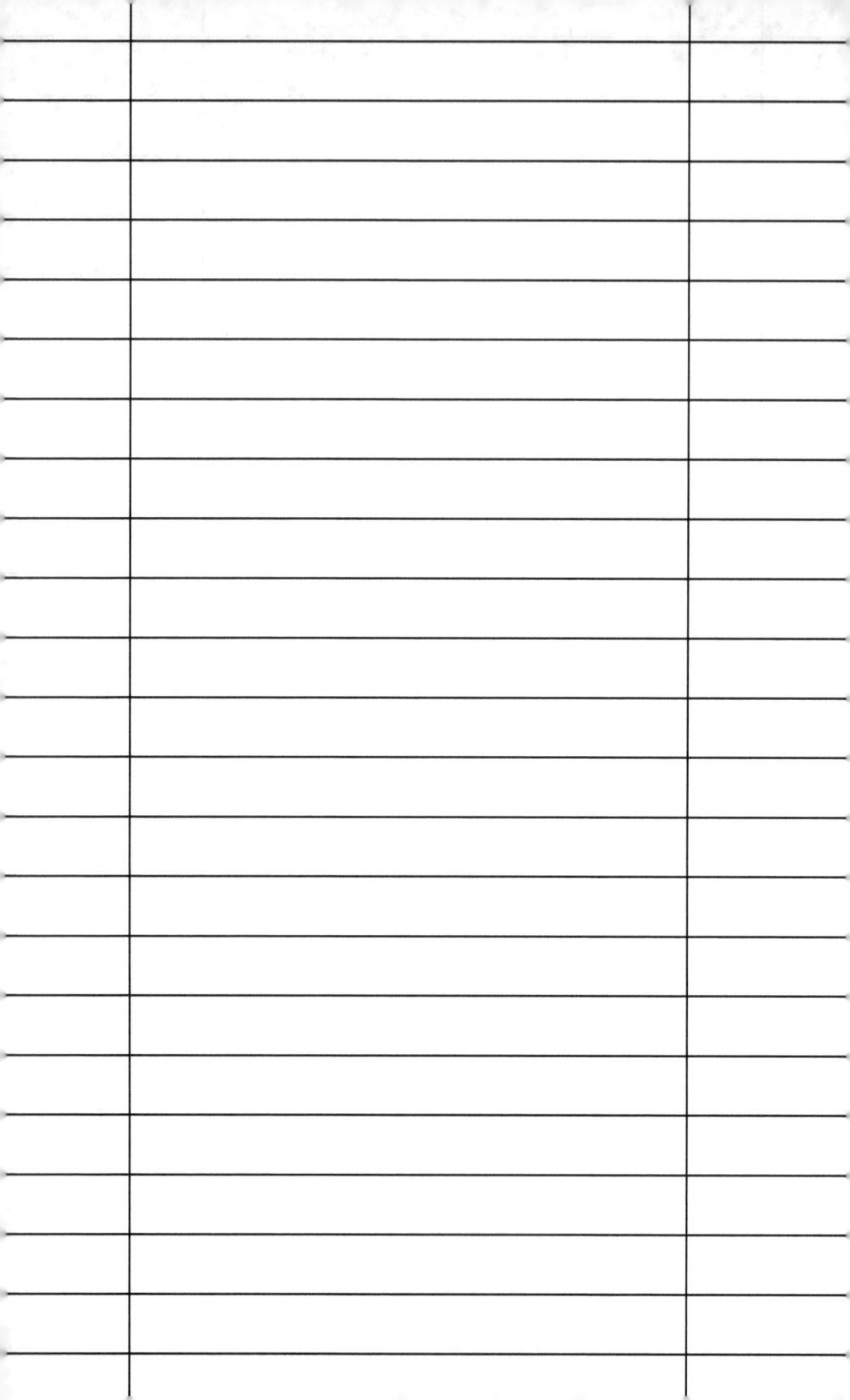

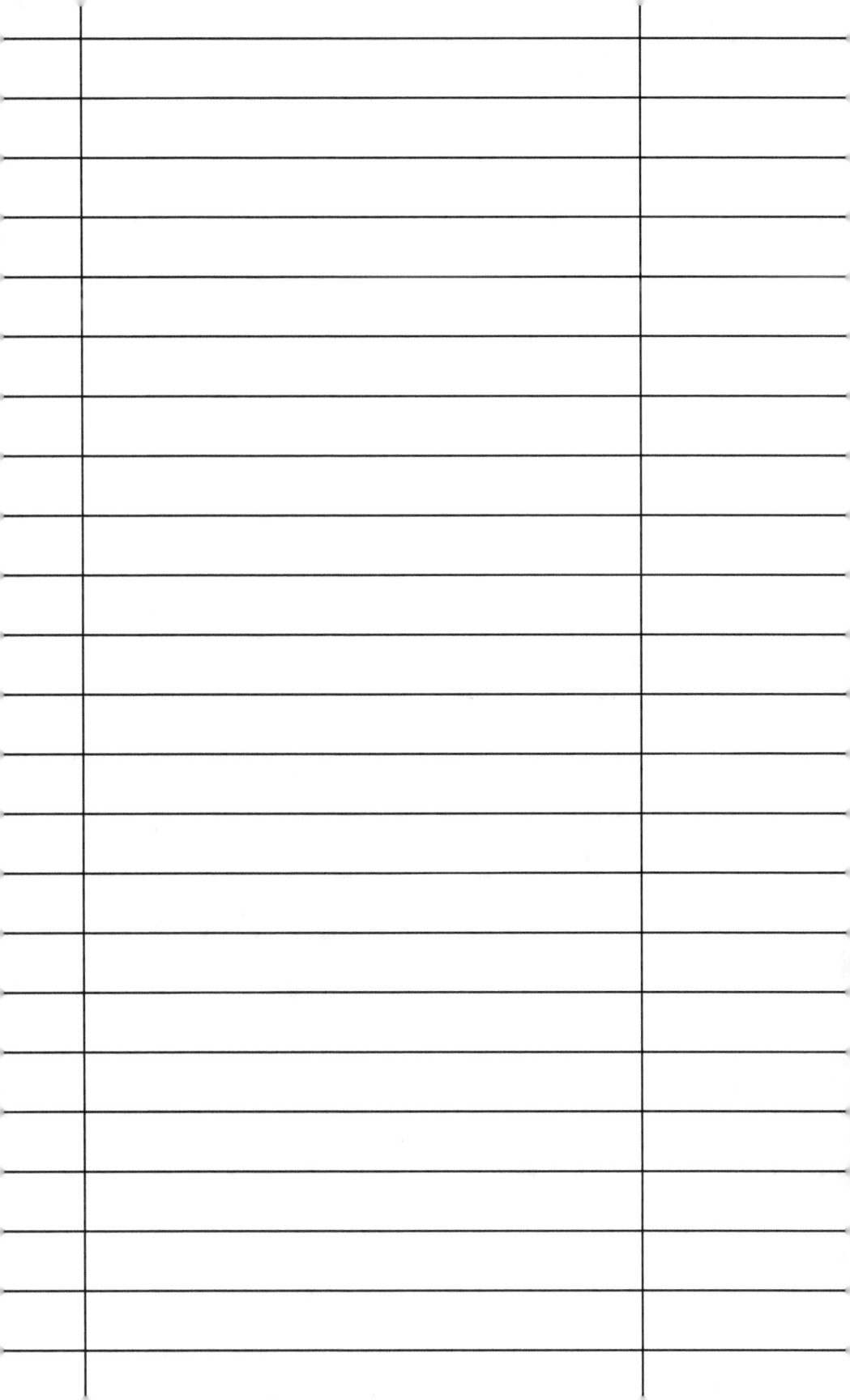

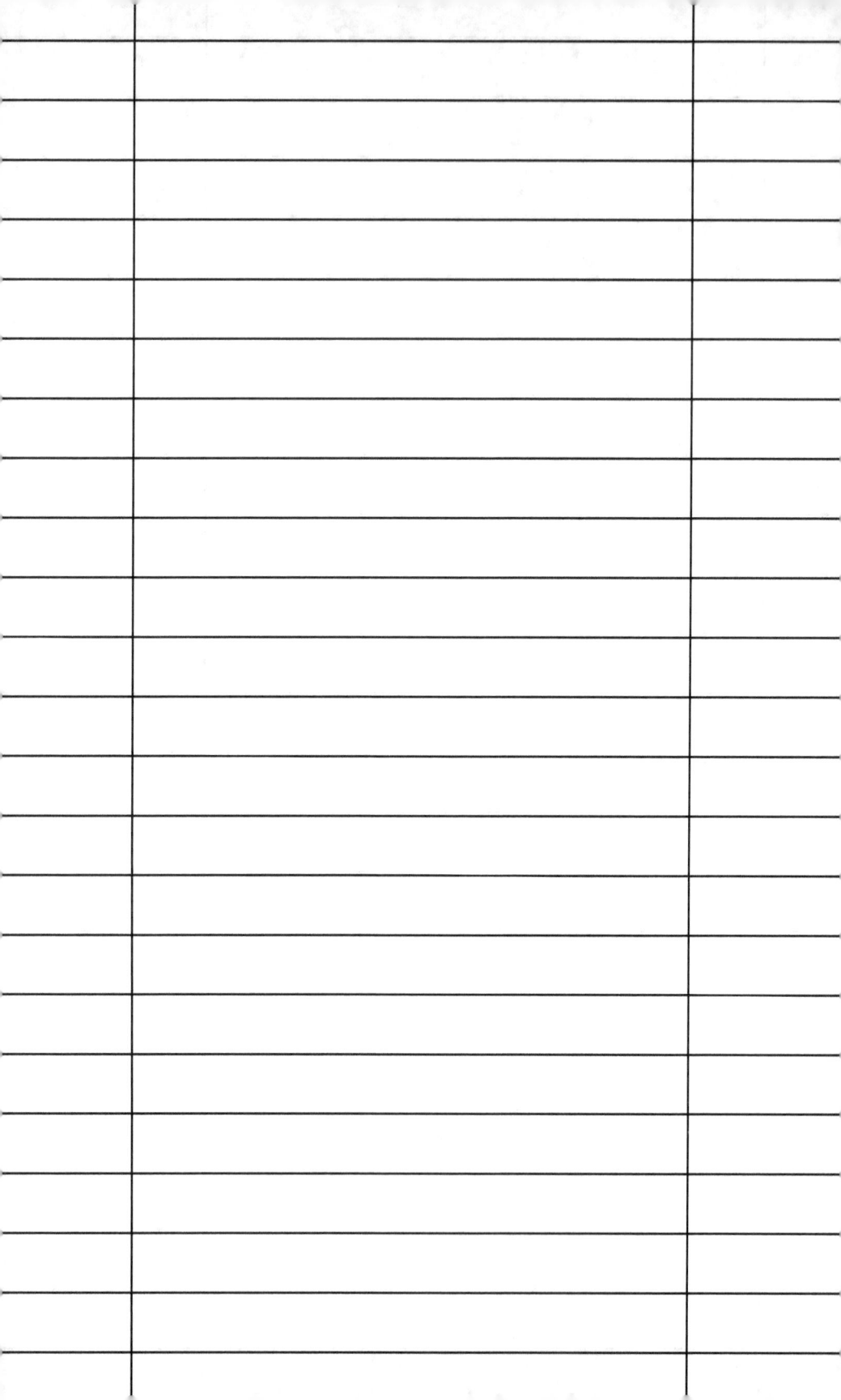

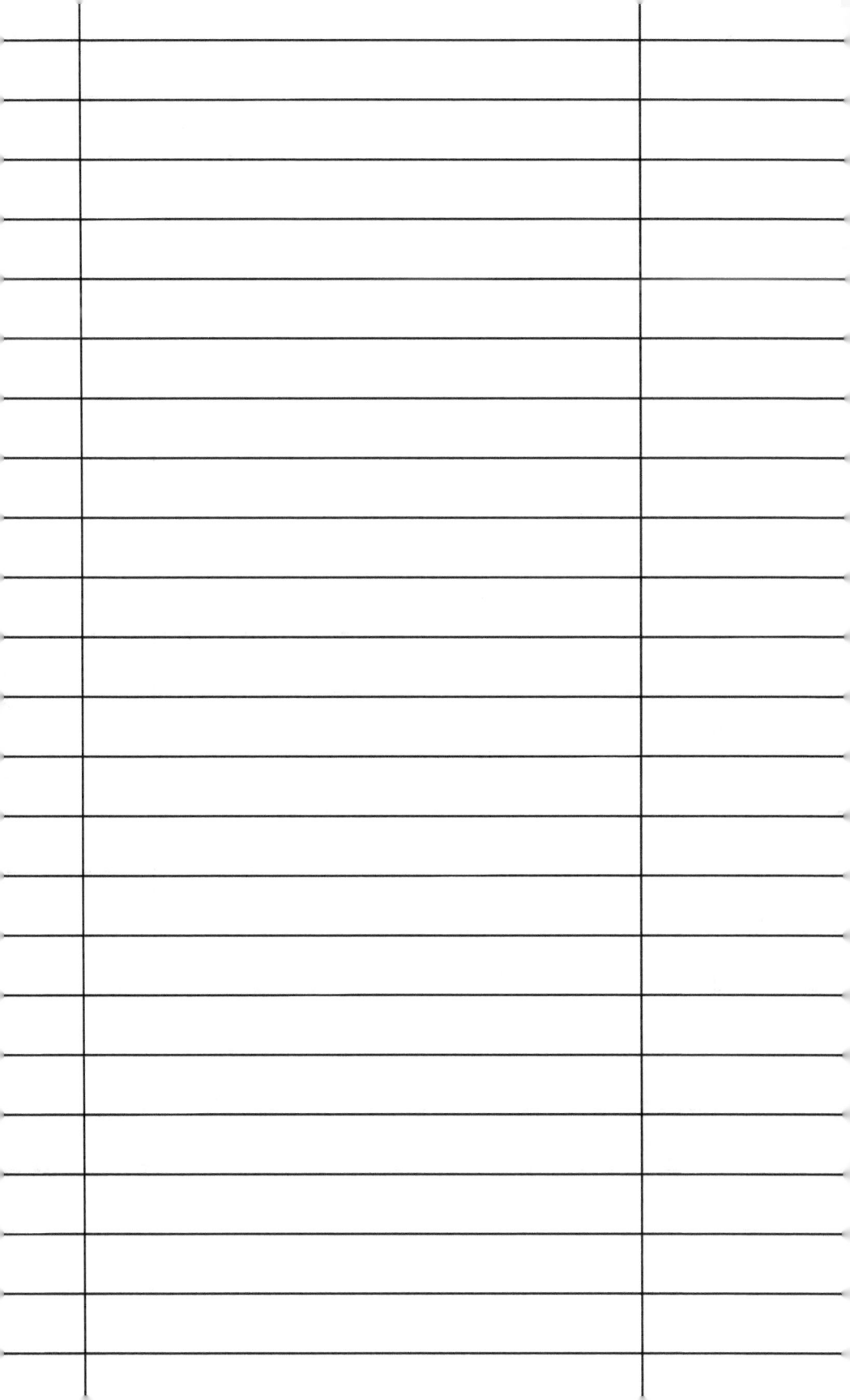

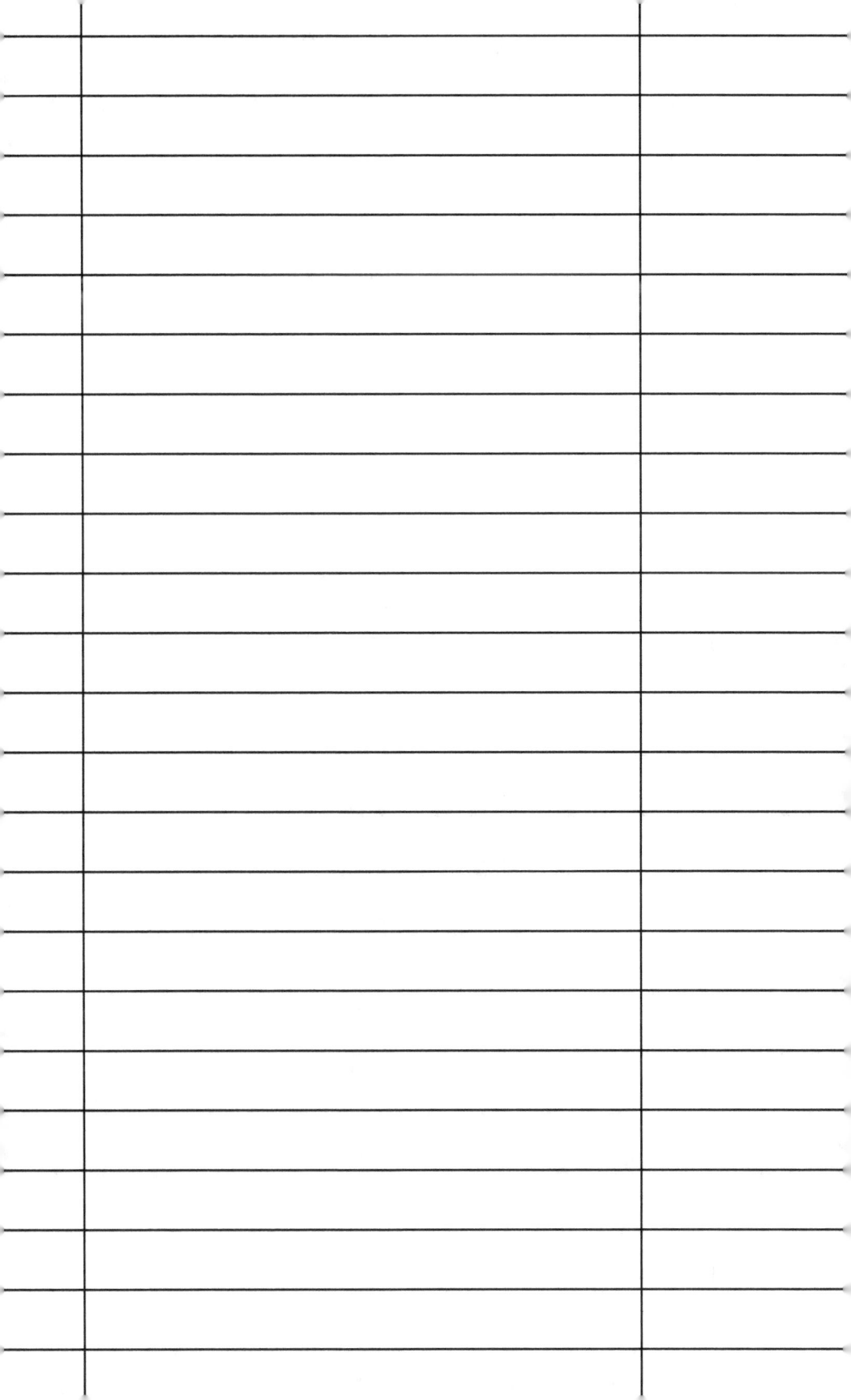

)ject

ription :

Date | Total Budget

	Expented Cost	Actual Cost	Services	Expented Cost
al Cost			Total Cost	

s :

Project

Description :

| on Date | | Total Budget | |

List	Expented Cost	Actual Cost	Services	Expented Cost
Total Cost			Total Cost	

Notes :

oject

cription :

Date **Total Budget**

Expented Cost	Actual Cost	Services	Expented Cost

al Cost | | **Total Cost** |

es :

Project

Description :

on Date **Total Budget**

List	Expented Cost	Actual Cost	Services	Expented Cost
Total Cost			**Total Cost**	

otes :

ject

ription :

Date   Total Budget

Expented Cost	Actual Cost	Services	Expented Cost
al Cost		Total Cost	

s :

Project	

Description :

on Date		Total Budget	

List	Expented Cost	Actual Cost	Services	Expented C
Total Cost			Total Cost	

Notes :

ject

ription :

Date **Total Budget**

Expented Cost	Actual Cost	Services	Expented Cost

al Cost | | **Total Cost** |

s :

Project

escription :

on Date   **Total Budget**

List	Expented Cost	Actual Cost	Services	Expented C
Total Cost			**Total Cost**	

otes :

bject				

ription :

Date		Total Budget	

	Expented Cost	Actual Cost	Services	Expented Cost
al Cost			Total Cost	

es :

Project

escription :

on Date   Total Budget

List	Expented Cost	Actual Cost		Services	Expented Co
Total Cost				**Total Cost**	

otes :

ject

ription :

Date   Total Budget

Expented Cost	Actual Cost	Services	Expented Cost

al Cost   Total Cost

s :

Project

Description :

on Date		Total Budget	

List	Expented Cost	Actual Cost	Services	Expented C
Total Cost			**Total Cost**	

otes :

)ject

ription :

Date		Total Budget	

	Expented Cost	Actual Cost	Services	Expented Cost
al Cost			Total Cost	

s :

Project

escription :

on Date   Total Budget

List	Expented Cost	Actual Cost	Services	Expented C
Total Cost			Total Cost	

otes :

bject

cription :

Date | Total Budget

Expented Cost	Actual Cost	Services	Expented Cost
al Cost		Total Cost	

es :

Project

escription :

on Date　　　　　　**Total Budget**

.ist	Expented Cost	Actual Cost	Services	Expented Co
otal Cost			**Total Cost**	

otes :

ject	
ription :	

Date		Total Budget	

Expented Cost	Actual Cost	Services	Expented Cost
al Cost		**Total Cost**	

s :

Project

Description :

| on Date | | Total Budget | |

List	Expented Cost	Actual Cost	Services	Expented Cost
Total Cost			**Total Cost**	

Notes :

oject	
ription :	

Date		Total Budget	

Expented Cost	Actual Cost	Services	Expented Cost
al Cost		Total Cost	

s :

Project

escription :

on Date   Total Budget

List	Expented Cost	Actual Cost	Services	Expented C
Total Cost			Total Cost	

otes :

bject

cription :

Date　　　　　　　　**Total Budget**

Expented Cost	Actual Cost	Services	Expented Cost
al Cost		**Total Cost**	

s :

Project

escription :

on Date   **Total Budget**

List	Expented Cost	Actual Cost	Services	Expented Co
Total Cost			**Total Cost**	

otes :

ject

ription :

Date **Total Budget**

Expented Cost	Actual Cost	Services	Expented Cost
al Cost		**Total Cost**	

s :

Project	
Description :	

on Date		Total Budget	

List	Expented Cost	Actual Cost	Services	Expented C
Total Cost			Total Cost	

otes :

ject

 ription :

 Date | Total Budget

Expented Cost	Actual Cost	Services	Expented Cost
al Cost		Total Cost	

 s :

Project	

escription :

on Date		Total Budget	

List	Expented Cost	Actual Cost	Services	Expented C
Total Cost			Total Cost	

otes :

bject	
cription :	

Date		Total Budget	

	Expented Cost	Actual Cost	Services	Expented Cost
al Cost			Total Cost	

es :

Project

escription :

on Date   Total Budget

ist	Expented Cost	Actual Cost	Services	Expented Co
otal Cost			Total Cost	

otes :

	ject		

ription :

Date		Total Budget	

Expented Cost	Actual Cost	Services	Expented Cost
al Cost		**Total Cost**	

:s :

Project

Description :

| on Date | | Total Budget | |

List	Expented Cost	Actual Cost	Services	Expented Cost
Total Cost			**Total Cost**	

Notes :

ject

ription :

Date		Total Budget	

	Expented Cost	Actual Cost	Services	Expented Cost
al Cost			Total Cost	

s :

Project	

Description :

on Date		Total Budget	

List	Expented Cost	Actual Cost	Services	Expented C...
Total Cost			**Total Cost**	

Notes :

bject	
cription :	

Date		Total Budget	

Expented Cost	Actual Cost	Services	Expented Cost
al Cost		Total Cost	

es :

Project

escription :

on Date   **Total Budget**

.ist	Expented Cost	Actual Cost	Services	Expented Co
otal Cost			Total Cost	

otes :

ject

ription :

Date　　　　　　　　　　**Total Budget**

Expented Cost	Actual Cost	Services	Expented Cost
al Cost		**Total Cost**	

es :

Project	
escription :	

on Date		Total Budget	

List	Expented Cost	Actual Cost	Services	Expented C
Total Cost			**Total Cost**	

otes :

bject

ription :

Date **Total Budget**

Expented Cost	Actual Cost	Services	Expented Cost

al Cost **Total Cost**

es :

Project

escription :

on Date   Total Budget

List	Expented Cost	Actual Cost	Services	Expented C
otal Cost			**Total Cost**	

otes :

bject

cription :

Date   Total Budget

Expented Cost	Actual Cost	Services	Expented Cost

al Cost   Total Cost

es :

Project

scription :

on Date   **Total Budget**

ist	Expented Cost	Actual Cost	Services	Expented Co
otal Cost				Total Cost

otes :

oject

ription :

Date   **Total Budget**

Expented Cost	Actual Cost	Services	Expented Cost

al Cost   **Total Cost**

s :

Project	

Description :

on Date		Total Budget	

List	Expented Cost	Actual Cost	Services	Expented Cost
Total Cost			**Total Cost**	

Notes :